GALE
CENGAGE Learning

Drama for Students, Volume 2

Staff

David Galens and Lynn M. Spampinato, *Editors*

Thomas Allbaugh, Craig Bentley, Terry Browne, Christopher Busiel, Stephen Coy, L. M. Domina, John Fiero, Carol L. Hamilton, Erika Kreger, Jennifer Lewin, Sheri Metzger, Daniel Moran, Terry Nienhuis, Bonnie Russell, Arnold Schmidt, William Wiles, Joanne Woolway, *Contributing Writers*

Elizabeth Cranston, Kathleen J. Edgar, Joshua Kondek, Marie Lazzari, Tom Ligotti, Marie Napierkowski, Scot Peacock, Mary Ruby, Diane Telgen, Patti Tippett, Kathleen Wilson, Pam Zuber, *Contributing Editors*

Pamela Wilwerth Aue, *Managing Editor*

Jeffery Chapman, *Programmer/Analyst*

Victoria B. Cariappa, *Research Team Manager*
Michele P. LaMeau, Andy Guy Malonis, Barb

McNeil, Gary Oudersluys, Maureen Richards, *Research Specialists*
Julia C. Daniel, Tamara C. Nott, Tracie A. Richardson, Cheryl L. Warnock, *Research Associates*

Susan M. Trosky, *Permissions Manager*
Kimberly F. Smilay, *Permissions Specialist*
Sarah Chesney, *Permissions Associate*
Steve Cusack, Kelly A. Quin, *Permissions Assistants*

Mary Beth Trimper, *Production Director*
Evi Seoud, *Assistant Production Manager*
Shanna Heilveil, *Production Assistant*

Randy Bassett, *Image Database Supervisor*
Mikal Ansari, Robert Duncan, *Imaging Specialists*
Pamela A. Reed, *Photography Coordinator*

Cynthia Baldwin, *Product Design Manager*
Cover design: Michelle DiMercurio, *Art Director*
Page design: Pamela A. E. Galbreath, *Senior Art Director*

Copyright © 1998
Gale Research
835 Penobscot Building
645 Griswold St.
Detroit, MI 48226-4094

ISBN 0-7876-1684-2

ISSN applied for and pending

Printed in the United States of America
10 9 8 7 6 5 4 3

A Raisin in the Sun

Lorraine Hansberry

1959

Introduction

A Raisin in the Sun was first produced in 1959 and anticipates many of the issues which were to divide American culture during the decade of the 1960s. Lorraine Hansberry, the playwright, was an unknown dramatist who achieved unprecedented success when her play became a Broadway sensation. Not only were successful women playwrights rare at the time, but successful young black women playwrights were virtually unheard of.

Within its context, the success of *A Raisin in the Sun* is particularly stunning.

In part because there were few black playwrights—as well as few black men and women who could attend Broadway productions—the play was hindered by a lack of financial support during its initial production. Producers hesitated to risk financial involvement in such an unprecedented event, for had the play been less well-written or well-acted, it could have suffered an incredible failure. Eventually, however, the play did find financial backing, and after staging initial performances in New Haven, Connecticut, it reached Broadway.

Compounding the racial challenges the play posed was its length of nearly three hours as it was originally written. Because audiences are not accustomed to plays of such length, especially by a newcomer, a couple of significant scenes were cut from the original production. (These scenes are sometimes included in later renditions.) These scenes include Walter's bedtime conversation with Travis and the family's interaction with Mrs. Johnson. In addition, the scene in which Beneatha appears with a "natural" haircut was eliminated in the original version primarily because Diana Sands, the actress, was not attractive enough with this haircut to reinforce the point of the scene. This scene would become more crucial as cultural ideas shifted.

Author Biography

Born in Chicago in 1930, Lorraine Hansberry was the youngest of four children. Her father, Carl Hansberry, was a successful real estate agent—and his family hence middle-class—who bought a house in a previously all-white neighborhood when Lorraine was eight years old. His attempt to move his family into this home created much tension, since Chicago was then legally segregated. Subsequently, however, as a result of Carl Hansberry's lawsuit, the Illinois Supreme Court declared these housing segregation laws unconstitutional.

After high school Hansberry attended the University of Wisconsin, where she studied drama, and the Art Institute of Chicago, where she studied painting. She moved to New York in 1950, supporting herself through a variety of jobs including work as a reporter and editor, while she continued to write short stories and plays. Before completing *A Raisin in the Sun,* she attempted three plays and a novel. During this period, she also met and married her husband, Robert Nemiroff, a white man who shared Hansberry's political perspective. They were divorced in 1964.

When Hansberry began *A Raisin in the Sun,* she titled it *The Crystal Stair,* which is also a line in a poem by Langston Hughes. The eventual title under which the play was and is performed is taken from Hughes's famous "A Dream Deferred." The play achieved its Broadway debut in 1959—it was the first play by a black woman to be produced in a Broadway theater. Several other "firsts" occurred because of this production; for example, Hansberry was the youngest playwright and first black playwright to win the New York Drama Critics Circle Award. This was a particularly rewarding honor, since Eugene O'Neill and Tennessee Williams, two of America's most prominent playwrights, also had plays on Broadway at this time. This version of *Raisin in the Sun* ran for 530 performances. A film version for which Hansberry had written the screen-play was also released in 1961. She was nominated for the Screen Writers Guild award for her work.

Hansberry began another play, *The Sign in Sidney Brustein's Window*. Although it was less successful, it ran on Broadway for 101 performances. It closed on the day of Hansberry's death, January 12, 1965. At the age of 35, after a remarkably brief illness, Hansberry died of cancer.

Act I, Scene One

The opening scene of *A Raisin in the Sun* occurs on a Friday morning when the members of the Younger family are preparing to go to school or work. During this scene, as in the opening scene of most plays, several key pieces of information are revealed. The family's inadequate living situation is conveyed through the fact that they share a bathroom with other tenants in their apartment house and through the fact that Travis must sleep on the sofa in the living room. As crucial, Walter's conversation elicits the fact that Mama is expecting a significant check in the mail the following day— life insurance paid to them because Mama's husband and Walter and Beneatha's father has died. The tension over money is also evident when Ruth refuses to give Travis fifty cents he needs for school. Walter gives him the money, along with an additional fifty cents to demonstrate that the family is not as poor as Ruth claims. Ironically, however, when Walter leaves for work, he will have to ask Ruth for carfare since he has given all his money to Travis.

During breakfast, Walter discusses the liquor store he wants to buy with the money Mama will receive. The other family members are hesitant to invest money with Walter's friends. Walter becomes increasingly frustrated, but when he expresses his longing for a more independent life and a career beyond that of chauffeur for a white man, Ruth and Beneatha discount his desires. Beneatha reminds him that the money belongs to Mama rather than directly to them, but her response is disingenuous because she already knows Mama plans to save some of the money for Beneatha's school tuition.

After the others leave, Ruth speaks to Mama about Walter's hopes. Mama is hesitant for at least two reasons—she does not approve of liquor, and she would like to buy a house for the family. This possibility excites Ruth, and within this conversation, Mama reveals why this dream is so significant to her. During this conversation, Beneatha states that she has another date with George Murchison, a young man she doesn't particularly like. This puzzles Mama since George comes from a wealthy family. The conversation grows more tense, however, when Beneatha defies her mother regarding religion, making statements Mama considers to be blasphemous. The scene concludes when Ruth suddenly faints, an act that will be explained later.

Act I, Scene Two

This scene occurs the following morning, with most of the family cleaning house and waiting for the mailman. Ruth, however, has gone out, and Mama implies that it might be because she's pregnant. Beneatha states that she's about to receive a visitor, Joseph Asagai, from Nigeria. There follows a discussion of European colonialism in Africa—although Mama appears somewhat ignorant, Beneatha's knowledge seems particularly new and her attitude self-righteous. At this point, Ruth returns and confirms that she is pregnant. Although Mama is pleased, Ruth and Beneatha think of the child as simply another financial burden.

They are diverted from their conversation when Beneatha spies Travis outside chasing a rat with his friends. During this confused moment, Asagai arrives. He critiques Beneatha because she has straightened her hair according to the style of the time. He suggests that she is a racial assimilationist—that is, that she aspires to white values. Simultaneously, he asserts that a woman's primary sense of fulfillment should come from her role as a wife.

After Asagai leaves, the mailman arrives with the check. Walter returns home, more frustrated than ever, especially when Mama urges him to go talk to Ruth. Mama is concerned because Walter is going "outside his home to look for peace" and because the "doctor" Ruth has gone to see is an abortionist. Although she expects Walter to be outraged at this possibility, he seems by his silence to agree that abortion would not be such a bad idea.

Act II, Scene One

Later that day, Beneatha appears in an African gown Asagai has given her. Walter is drunk and wants to act like an African warrior. George Murchison arrives to pick up Beneatha, but he is displeased at her appearance and refuses to take her seriously. She is, he says, "eccentric." Walter responds to George antagonistically, describing him as wearing "faggoty-looking white shoes." Ruth understands that something has gone drastically wrong, and that whatever she and Walter once shared, that love is gone.

Mama returns home, stating that she has been doing business downtown. She has in fact bought a house—located in Clybourne Park, an entirely white neighborhood. She bought that house not because she wanted to make a political statement but because it was big enough for her family and within her price range.

Act II, Scene Two

In this scene, Mrs. Johnson, a neighbor, arrives, ostensibly to congratulate the Youngers on their impending move. Within the conversation, however, she brings up recent bombings of houses belonging to black families moving into previously all-white neighborhoods. Within this conversation, Mama reveals herself to have more militant feelings than she had previously expressed. When Walter confesses that he has not been to work for three days, Mama begins to rethink her decision and eventually offers some of the money to Walter so that he can buy the liquor store and "be the head of this family from now on like you supposed to be."

Act II, Scene Three

At this point, the family mood has improved considerably. Ruth and Walter have gone to the movies for the first time in years, and Ruth has bought curtains for the new house. In the midst of their excitement, a white man knocks at their door, introducing himself as Karl Lindner, from the "New Neighbors Orientation Committee." Although he attempts to present himself not as racist but merely reasonable, his goal is to buy the house back from the Youngers, who refuse his offer. After he leaves, Beneatha asks, "What they think we going to do— eat 'em?" Ruth responds, "No, honey, marry 'em."

To celebrate their good fortune, the family has bought Mama a set of gardening tools, but in the midst of their celebration, Bobo, a friend of Walter's arrives. He reveals that Willy, their mutual friend and potential business partner, has disappeared with all of their money. Mama is especially outraged because the money represented everything for which her husband had suffered. The scene ends with the family as dejected as they had been joyous at the beginning.

Act III

Walter has gone to Karl Lindner's apparently to accept his offer, but when Lindner arrives, the family has regained its determination to move. The movers arrive. The play concludes on an ambiguous note—for although the family is moving, their life in Clybourne Park will likely be difficult.

Joseph Asagai

Joseph Asagai is a friend of Beneatha's who has been out of town all summer. He is from Nigeria and introduces Beneatha to Nigerian culture. He brings her a native African dress, for example, and also encourages her to let her hair grow naturally rather than have it straightened—although this encouragement is phrased in terms of an insult. He, in other words, introduces issues that would become prominent in the United States during the decade following the production of this play (issues related to African American pride and heritage). On the other hand, he discourages Beneatha from acting independently as a woman, arguing that the only true feeling a woman should have is passion for her husband.

Bobo

Bobo is an extremely minor character. He appears near the end of the scene to convey the bad news that his and Walter's friend has absconded with their money. He feels as dejected as Walter since the amount of money he had contributed consisted of his entire savings.

Mrs. Johnson

Mrs. Johnson is a neighbor of the Youngers, and she is portrayed as nosy and manipulative. In her primary scene, she appears to be jealous of the Youngers's good fortune and seems to want to ruin it for them by raising their fears. In some versions of this play, her role is eliminated.

Karl Lindner

Karl is a white man and the represent of the Neighborhood Welcoming Committee for Clybourne Park, where the Youngers plan to move. Although Karl attempts to present himself as a reasonable man, he has racist motives in attempting to persuade the Youngers not to move to his neighborhood. Although he himself might not commit violence, his goals are consistent with those who would commit violence in order to keep neighborhoods segregated.

Mama

See Lena Younger

George Murchison

George is Beneatha's date, though she doesn't take him seriously as a future mate. In the elder Youngers's eyes, his primary attractive quality is his access to wealth. Yet his presence also raises the issue of class tensions within the black community. He claims to have no interest in African culture and is exactly the opposite of the idealist Joseph Asagai.

Beneatha Younger

Beneatha is the younger sister of Walter, the daughter of Mama, sister-in-law of Ruth, and aunt of Travis. Throughout the play, she struggles for an adult identity, determined to express her ideas but often failing to do so tactfully. She dates a wealthy college friend, George Murchison, whom she describes as boring, in part because he is so conventional. She is also interested in Joseph Asagai, another college acquaintance whose home is Nigeria. She eventually follows his desire that she should adopt a more native African style. Also significant to the play is her desire to be a doctor, a goal for which she will need some of the money Mama has inherited.

Lena Younger

Mama's role in the play is quite significant. She is a woman with dreams but also with the wisdom to know when to act on them. She receives a $10,000 insurance payment as a result of her husband's death and longs to buy a more comfortable house for her family. Yet when she realizes how much a business would mean to Walter, she gives him a substantial portion of the money, hoping this will encourage him to live more fully. She is also, however, a woman of strong conviction, as is apparent in the scene when Beneatha suggests that God is imaginary but more significantly in the scene when Walter seems to agree with Ruth regarding the abortion. At this point, she recognizes that her family's enemy has been transferred from their culture to their own hearts. Mama is clearly the source of the family's strength as well as its soul.

Ruth Younger

Ruth is married to Walter and hence the daughter-in-law of Mama and sister-in-law of Beneatha. She is the mother of Travis. She clearly loves her husband and family but also clearly feels the stress of poverty. Although she is enthusiastic about the family owning its own home, she urges Mama to help Walter invest in the liquor store because it means so much to him. During the course of the play, Ruth realizes she is pregnant and considers seeking an abortion, which would have been illegal at the time. By the end of the play, the implication is that Ruth will have this baby and that the family will direct its energy away from self-destruction.

Travis Younger

Travis is the son of Walter and Ruth. His role in the play is minor; he serves primarily as a foil permitting the other characters to raise the issues of the play. He is at the cusp of adolescence, simultaneously attempting stereotypic adult masculine reticence and longing for childlike affection. He is received affectionately by the other characters.

Media Adaptations

- *A Raisin in the Sun* was released as a film by Columbia Pictures in 1961. Its cast included Sidney Poitier, Ruby Dee, Claudia McNeil, Diana Sands, and Louis Gossett Jr. This version was produced by David Susskind and Philip Rose. This film is distributed by Columbia Tristar Home Video.

- An American Playhouse version of the play was released for television in 1989. It is distributed through Fries Home Video and stars Danny Glover, Esther Rolle, and Starletta DuPois, and is directed by Bill Duke.

- Another video which was originally a filmstrip provides a supplment to the play. It is also called *A Raisin in the Sun* and is available from Afro-American Distributing Company.

- A cassette sound recording of the play is available from Harper Audio. It stars Ossie Davis, Ruby Dee, Claudia McNeil, Diana Sands, and Lloyd Richards. This cassette was produced in 1972.

Walter Lee Younger

Walter is the son of Mama, the husband of Ruth, the brother of Beneatha, and the father of Travis. He works as a chauffeur, a job he finds unsatisfying on a number of levels but most particularly because he does not desire to be anyone's servant. Although he is in his mid-thirties, his living situation encourages him to believe he is perceived nearly as a child. He longs to invest his father's insurance money in a liquor store because he wants to achieve financial success through his own efforts. When his friend runs off with the money, Walter feels particularly hopeless. Ironically, however, he achieves a sense of himself as an adult and leader of his family in part through this event. By standing up to Karl Lindner when it would have been easier to accept Lindner's financial offer, Walter asserts himself forcefully into his culture—and although his choices may make his life difficult in some ways, he will not be spiritually defeated.

Race and Racism

The clear primary theme of A *Raisin in the Sun* has to do with race and racism. The Youngers live in a segregated neighborhood in a city that remains one of the most segregated in the United States. Virtually every act they perform is affected by their race. Ruth is employed as a domestic servant and Walter as a chauffeur in part because they are black —they are the servants, that is, of white people. They are limited to their poorly maintained apartment in part because they have low-paying jobs but also because absentee landlords often do not maintain their property. Travis chases a rat, while Beneatha and Mama attempt to eradicate cockroaches, both activities which would not occur in wealthier neighborhoods.

The most significant scene which openly portrays racism, however, is the visit with Karl Lindner. Although he does not identify himself as racist, and although his tactics are less violent than some, he wants to live in an all-white neighborhood —and he is willing to pay the Youngers off to stay out of white neighborhoods. This type of racism is often dangerous because it is more easily hidden.

Prejudice and Tolerance

Closely related to the theme of race and racism is the theme of prejudice and tolerance. Karl Lindner and his neighbors are clearly prejudiced against black people. Yet other forms of prejudice and intolerance also surface in the play. Walter responds to George Murchison aggressively because George is wealthy and educated; educated men seem to Walter somehow less masculine. Similarly, although Joseph Asagai encourages Beneatha to feel proud of her racial identity, he discourages her from feeling proud of her intellectual abilities because he believes professional achievements are irrelevant to a proper woman.

Civil Rights

Also related to the theme of race and racism as well as to the theme of prejudice and tolerance is the theme of Civil Rights. Although this play would debut before the major Civil Rights movement occurred in the United States during the 1960s, it raises many of the issues that would eventually be raised by the larger culture."Civil Rights" generally refer to the rights a person has by law—such as the right to vote or the right to attend an adequate schools—and are often also referred to as human rights. The central civil rights issue in this play is, of course, the idea of segregated housing. Mama Younger has the money to pay for a house she wants, but people attempt to prevent her from doing so because of her race. At this moment, she is not trying to make a political point but rather to purchase the best house available for the money.

Houses available in her own ghetto neighborhood are both more costly and less well-kept.

American Dream

The "American Dream" includes many ideas, but it is primarily the belief that anyone who comes to or is born in America can achieve success through hard work. Walter Younger aspires to achieve part of this American Dream, but he is frustrated at every turn. Although he is willing to work hard, opportunities for him are few because he is black. His culture has relegated him to the servant class. When some money does become available to him, his business opportunities are also few—for few businesses historically thrived in minority neighborhoods. Yet by the end of the play, whether or not he achieves the American Dream, he does achieve a sense of himself as an individual with power and the ability to make choices.

Sex Roles

While questions of race are certainly prominent in the play, an equally significant, if less prominent, issue involves gender. Mama understands that in order to experience himself as an adult, Walter must experience himself as a man —that is, he must be the leader of a family. Of course, in order for Walter to be the leader, the women must step back. And even within their stations as servants, Walter and Ruth's roles are further divided according to their sex—Walter is the chauffeur, Ruth the domestic servant. More blatantly, however, Joseph Asagai asserts that women have only one role in life—that of wife and presumably mother. And although Beneatha longs to be a doctor, she is also caught up in the romance of potentially being Asagai's wife. This tension points out the fact that individuals can be exceptionally progressive in one area of their lives while being much less progressive in other areas.

Topics for Further Study

- Research segregation laws that applied to various U.S. cities in the 1950s. Examine the arguments people made in efforts to change these laws.

- Investigate the history of a particular neighborhood with which you are familiar. Analyze how its ethnic composition has shifted over decades or centuries and discuss the causes and effects of those shifts.

- Write an argument for or against owning or investing in a liquor store. Try to use specific examples or statistics in your essay. Consider the ethical as well as economic issues involved.

- Research the recent history of Nigeria. Compare its national events with the predictions Joseph Asagai makes in the play.

- Compare how extended families functioned in the 1950's (or another time period of your choice) with the way they function today.

Style

Setting

Among the most important elements of *A Raisin in the Sun* is its setting. Because the Youngers are attempting to buy a new home in a different neighborhood, their current apartment and neighborhood achieve particular significance. The play takes place in a segregated Chicago neighborhood, "sometime between World War II and the present," which for Hansberry would be the late 1950s. In other words, the play occurs during the late 1940s or the 1950s, a time when many Americans were prosperous and when some racial questions were beginning to be raised, but before the Civil Rights movement of the 1960s.

More specifically, the play occurs in the Youngers' apartment, which Hansberry describes in detail: "Its furnishings are typical and undistinguished and their primary feature now is that they have clearly had to accomodate the living of too many people for too many years." The furnishings, that is, come to represent the hard lives of the characters, for though everything is regularly cleaned, the furniture is simply too old and worn to bring joy or beauty into the Youngers' lives, except in their memories. Other details of the setting also contribute to this closed-in feeling: the couch which serves as Travis's bed, the bathroom which must be shared with the neighbors.

Allusion

Two significant allusions are prominent in this play—one literary and one historical. The title of the play, *A Raisin in the Sun,* is taken from a poem by Langston Hughes, "Harlem." Langston Hughes was a prominent African American poet during the Harlem Renaissance, a period during the 1920s when many African American writers achieved considerable stature. The poem asks whether a dream deferred, or put off, dries up "like a raisin in the sun" or whether it explodes. During the play, Mama realizes that some members of her family are drying up, while others such as Walter are about to explode, and she realizes that their dreams can be deferred no longer.

The other major allusion is to Booker T. Washington, who is quoted by Mrs. Johnson as saying "Education has spoiled many a good plow hand." Booker T. Washington was a prominent African American during the late nineteenth century; perhaps his most well-known speech is his "Atlanta Exposition Address." Washington argued that Negroes should not aspire to academic education but should learn trades such as mechanics and farming instead. He also suggested that Negroes should not agitate for political rights and that while the races might intermingle for business purposes, they should live separate social lives. His primary opponent during this time was W. E. B. DuBois, who argued for equality and desegregation. Within the context of the play, Washington is understood as a negative example.

Climax

The climax of a work of literature occurs at the point when the tension can get no greater and the conflicts must resolve. In longer works, there may be several points of heightened tension before the final resolution. The climax of *A Raisin in the Sun* occurs when Karl Lindner visits the house for the second time, when Walter is about to accept his offer but changes his mind. The audience understands that while the Youngers may now achieve their dreams, their lives in this racist culture will remain difficult.

Foreshadowing

Foreshadowing occurs when a later event is hinted at earlier in the work. This occurs in *A Raisin in the Sun* when Ruth faints at the end of Scene One. This is a standard, almost stereotypic, way to convey pregnancy, which Ruth will confirm later in the play—and which will become significant through the family's response to it.

Symbolism

A symbol is an object that has value in itself but also represents an idea—something concrete, in other words, that represents something abstract. One of the symbols in *A Raisin in the Sun* is Mama's straggly plant. She wants to take this to the new house, although she plans to have a much more successful garden there, because this plant "expresses ME." Though the plant has struggled to live and seems to lack the beauty for which it would ordinarily be valued, it is significant to Mama because it has survived despite the struggle, as her family has survived.

The Civil Rights Movement of the 1950s

A Raisin in the Sun directly addresses the issue of segregated housing in the United States. While many neighborhoods remain effectively segregated today, such segregation was legally enforced during the 1950s. Despite several Constitutional Amendments subsequent to the Civil War, African Americans were denied many civil rights a full century later. In 1954, the case of Brown vs. Board of Education was tried in Kansas; it reached the United States Supreme Court in 1955. The Court found that segregated education was inherently unequal education, effectively outlawing the practice of "separate but equal" school systems. Also in 1955, the Montgomery bus boycott occurred, with blacks and some whites refusing to ride city buses that forced blacks to sit in the back. In 1958, the public schools in Little Rock, Arkansas were closed by the Governor in an attempt to defy the Supreme Court's ruling. In 1959, the bus system of Atlanta, Georgia, was integrated, although the Governor asked riders to continue "voluntary" segregation. Ironically, in that same year, the United Nations voted to condemn racial discrimination anywhere in the world. By the 1960s, Civil Rights demonstrations became common and resulted in much new legislation, although cultural implementation of those ideas would take much longer.

Compare & Contrast

- **1950s:** Schools and neighborhoods were racially (and sometimes ethnically) segregated, often by law. These laws received several major court challenges during this decade; many of the laws were declared unconstitutional.

  Today: Many neighborhoods and schools remain segregated despite legal and cultural attempts to reverse this situation. On the other hand, many schools, including prestigious universities, are completely integrated. Yet Affirmative Action, the practice through which this integration was in part achieved, is currently being challenged in several states.

- **1950s:** The computer microchip was invented by an employee of Texas Instruments and began to be widely produced. This invention would come to revolutionize the technological industry. Computers and computerized products were generally limited to military and industrial purposes and were not common household products. Computers that did exist were much larger than an average-sized living room.

Today: Nearly every American home contains one—or more likely several-products that rely on computer microprocessors. These include not only personal computers complete with modems but also digital watches and clocks, compact disc players, and remote control devices for televisions and videocassette recorders.

- **1950s:** Senator Joseph McCarthy held his famous Senate hearings which attempted to demonstrate Communist infiltration of many U.S. institutions, including the Army. Although he is eventually censured by the Senate, these hearings destroy the lives of many apparently innocent Americans.

Today: With the fall of the Berlin Wall, the demise of the Soviet Union, and the internal conflicts in many Eastern European countries, Communism is no longer perceived as a threat by most Americans. The United States has emerged as the single world superpower.

- **1950s:** Dr. Jonas Salk developed the polio vaccine; this and other medical advances significantly decreased the rate of childhood illness by the end of the decade.

  Today: Many childhood illnesses have been controlled in the United States, although the infant mortality rate remains comparatively high for a developed country. Other illnesses, however, such as cancer and AIDs (Acquired Immune Deficiency syndrome), have become more prominent and receive considerable attention within the medical community as well as within the general culture.

- **1950s:** The Universal Copyright Convention occurred when most Western nations agreed to protect the copyright of work produced in each other's countries. For example, a novel originally printed in England could not be reprinted in the United States without the author's permission.

  Today: Most nations respect the idea of copyright. However, the rise of the internet has complicated this issue, since it is now so easy to distribute copyrighted material in this new form. New laws are likely to be written regarding the electronic ownership of material.

Literature and Arts in the 1950s

Artistically and culturally, the 1950s are commonly thought of as a repressed decade, often with good reason. It wasn't until 1959, for example, that *Lady Chatterly's Lover* by D.H. Lawrence was permitted to be distributed in the United States. Definitions of obscenity shifted during this decade, as did many other cultural assumptions.

A Raisin in the Sun was only one of several significant plays which opened on Broadway during this period. Others include *Sweet Bird of Youth* by Tennessee Williams, *The Zoo Story* by Edward Albee, and *The Miracle Worker* by William Gibson. Musicals mat year included *Once upon a Mattress* starring Carol Burnett and *Gypsy* starring Ethel Merman and Jack Klugman. *The Sound of Music* also premiered starring Mary Martin.

Significant works also appeared in other forms of literature. E. B. White published his famous version of William Strunk's *The Elements of Style,* a grammar book that has become a standard in composition. Philip Roth published his collection of short stories, *Goodbye, Columbus,* while Saul Bellow published *Henderson the Rain King*. In Germany, Gunter Grass published his masterpiece, *The Tin Drum.*

Daily Life in the 1950s

Although the 1950s are known as a decade of prosperity, a significant number of Americans still lived in poverty. A study published by the University of Michigan demonstrated that 30% of families lived on or below the poverty line in 1959. In 1958, U.S. unemployment reached nearly 5.2 million. Simultaneously, some extremely wealthy Americans were able to avoid paying income taxes completely.

Because of technological discoveries, many aspects of daily life changed during the fifties. American automakers began to manufacture compact cars and computers began to be developed. Television became a popular source of home entertainment. People began to do the majority of their shopping at supermarkets rather than at small markets. Frozen orange juice concentrate became a popular item as did "heat and eat" frozen dinners (often called TV dinners).

Popular movies released in 1959 included *Ben Hur* starring Charlton Heston, Alfred Hitchcock's *North by Northwest* starring Cary Grant and Eva Marie Saint, and *The Diary of Anne Frank* with Millie Perkins and Shelley Winters. Rock and roll fans were saddened by the deaths of Buddy Holly and Ritchie Valens. Other musical performers included Paul Anka and Neil Sedaka. Perhaps the most famous toy ever—the Barbie doll—was also introduced this year; it would not be until 1968, however, that a black version of the doll would be produced.

Critical Overview

A Raisin in the Sun is easily Lorraine Hansberry's best-known work, although her early death is certainly a factor in her limited oeuvre. From its beginning, this play was critically and commercially successful. After a brief run in New Haven, Connecticut, it opened on Broadway in 1959, where it ran for 530 performances. Although this was the first play written by a black woman to appear on Broadway, it received the New York Drama Critics Circle Award. A later adaptation won a Tony Award for best musical in 1974.

Newspapers reviewers were lavish in their praise of this performance. According to Francis Dedmond in an article published in *American Playwrights since 1945,* various critics complimented the work's "moving story" and "dramatic impact" as well as the play's "honesty" and "real-life characters." Magazine writers were equally enthusiastic. According to an article in *Plays for the Theatre,* this play is "one of the best examples" of work produced by minority playwrights during the late 1950's and 1960's.

Because of this early success, the play was translated into more than thirty languages and performed on stage as well as over the radio in several countries. To celebrate its twenty-fifth anniversary in 1983 and 1984, several revivals occurred. Reviewers remained enthusiastic.

Critics agree that this is a realistic play that avoids stereotypic characters. This realism permitted the black characters to be understood and sympathized with by a primarily white audience. By avoiding extremist characters—by creating Karl Lindner as a nonviolent if prejudiced man rather than as a member of the Ku Klux Klan for example —Hansberry was able to persuade her audience of the constant if subtle presence and negative effects of racism. According to Glendyr Sacks in the *International Dictionary of Theatre-1: Plays,* "Interest in the play . . . was undoubtedly fuelled by the unusual experience, for a Broadway audience, of watching a play in which all but one character was black. Furthermore, the tone of the play was not didactic. Its values were familiar, . . . and to some extent audiences and critics, both predominantly white, must have felt some relief that the protest implicit in the play was not belligerent." While some contemporary critics would suggest that realism is outdated, others argue that the play's influence on subsequent black works has been highly pervasive. Literature can be politically and culturally challenging, in other words, even if its form is conventional. Because the play is not overt in its protest, some later critics viewed it as assimilationist, an ironic situation since the play itself protests against assimilationism.

Some critics, however, did critique *A Raisin in the Sun* for its realism. Gerald Weales, in an article published in *Commentary* in 1959, claimed that "The play, first of all, is old fashioned. Practically no serious playwright, in or out of America, works in such a determinedly naturalistic form." He continued, "in choosing to write such a play, she [Hansberry] entered Broadway's great sack race with only a paper bag as equipment." He also suggests that the plot is "mechanical" and "artificial." His criticism, however, seems to be primarily against the genre in general rather than against Hansberry's manipulation of it. The tone of this article indicates that no realistic play would win Weales's favor. By the end of his article, he does concede that *A Raisin in the Sun* is a good play with "genuinely funny and touching scenes throughout."

Hansberry herself responded to the reception of her play in an article she published in the *Village Voice* in 1959. She occasionally appeared amused at both the type and amount of response her play received. Some critics, she suggested, seem to think that any negative reaction at all would be inherently racist, while others seem to disdain emotional appeals in literature in general. On the other hand, she stated that the play has been "magnificently understood." She suggested that her characters choose life and hope despite the fact that the culture in general seems enamored with despair because the Youngers and people like them have had "'somewhere' they have been trying to get for so long that more sophisticated confusions do not yet bind them." Despair, in other words, is a luxury they cannot afford.

In part, though, this play remains popular specifically because of its realism. It presents characters whose values and goals are emotionally accessible to virtually any American audience, yet who through their eventual dignified responses to their situation achieve heroic status. Perhaps Hansberry's greatest contribution to subsequent drama was her ability to present black characters as admirable figures.

Further Reading

Dedmond, Francis. "Lorraine Hansberry" in *American Playwrights since 1945: A Guide to Scholarship, Criticism, and Performance,* edited by Philip C. Kolin, Greenwood, 1989, pp. 155-68.

> This is a thorough article which provides an assessment of Hansberry's reputation through her career. In addition, it includes a useful resource list.

Hansberry, Lorraine. "Willie Loman, Walter Younger, and He Who Must Live" in the *Village Voice,* Vol. IV, no. 42, August 12, 1959, pp. 7-8.

> Hansberry discusses positive and negative responses to her play and compares it to *Death of a Salesman* by Arthur Miller.

Howes, Kelly King, editor. "Lorraine Hansberry" in *Characters in 20th Century Literature, Book II,* Gale, 1995, pp. 204-09.

> This article approaches the play through an analysis of its characters. It provides an extensive discussion of each of the characters and compares them to other significant characters in American literature.

Sacks, Glendyr. "Raisin in the Sun" in *International Dictionary of Theatre-1: Plays,* edited by Mark

Hawkins-Dady, St. James Press, 1992, pp. 649-50.

> This article is a basic plot analysis which provides some cultural context.

Short, Hugh. "Lorraine Hansberry" in *Critical Survey of Drama,* edited by Frank Magill, Salem Press, 1994, pp. 1086-94.

> This article discusses *A Raisin in the Sun* in the context of Hansberry's other plays. Describing this play as the most successful, Short analyzes it according to its theme of heroism.

Wang, Qun. "A Raisin in the Sun" in *Reference Guide to American Literature,* edited by James Kamp, St. James Press, 1994, pp. 1031-32.

> This article briefly describes the major characters as well as situates Hansberry as a playwright within the canon of American literature.

Weales, Gerald. "Thoughts on *A Raisin in the Sun"* in *Commentary,* Vol. 27, no. 6, June, 1959, pp. 527-30.

> This review is among the more negative Hansberry received. Weales critiques the traditional form of the play, suggesting that the form guarantees stereotypes despite the qualities of the play that Weales himself praises.

CPSIA information can be obtained
at www.ICGtesting.com
Printed in the USA
LVOW13s1746311017
554455LV00010B/626/P